— PEOPLE TO KNOW —

JOHN LENNON
The Beatles and Beyond

David K. Wright

Enslow Publishers, Inc.

40 Industrial Road   PO Box 38
Box 398   Aldershot
Berkeley Heights, NJ 07922   Hants GU12 6BP
USA   UK

http://www.enslow.com

Library of Congress Cataloging-in-Publication Data

Wright, David K.
    John Lennon: the Beatles and beyond / David K. Wright.
       p. cm. — (People to know)
    Discography: p.
    Includes bibliographical references and index.
    Summary: Explores this rock musician's childhood and personal life, his career
with the Beatles and on his own, and his lasting impression on the music world.
    ISBN 0-89490-702-6
    1. Lennon, John, 1940–1980—Juvenile literature. 2. Rock
musicians—England—Biography—Juvenile literature. [1. Lennon, John,
1940–1980. 2. Musicians. 3. Rock music.] I. Title. II. Series.
ML3930.L34W75 1996
782.42166'092—dc20
   [B]   96-3345
                                     CIP
                                 AC MN

Printed in the United States of America

10 9 8 7 6 5

Illustration Credits:
UPI/Bettmann, pp. 35, 38, 45, 67, 73, 76, 78, 80, 89, 92, 99; Wisconsin
Center for Film and Theater Research, pp. 4, 49, 53, 54, 56, 59, 64.

Cover Illustration: UPI/Bettmann

Contents

John Lennon

1

The Beatles Take America

The Beatles, four young English musicians, were coming to America! Not since Elvis Presley sang and gyrated on network television nearly a decade earlier had rock 'n' roll made such news. The Beatles would perform in New York City on *The Ed Sullivan Show* on the CBS television network. The date was set for February 9, 1964, a Sunday evening.

Preshow publicity was staggering. Disc jockeys all across the country received kits that let them read a script, play a tape, and make it appear as if they were interviewing members of the shaggy-haired band on their local shows. Five million stickers stamped "THE BEATLES ARE COMING!" were distributed. By the end of January, "I Want to Hold Your Hand" had sold 2 million copies in the United States, and the band's album, *Meet the Beatles*, was climbing the charts.

Brian Epstein, the Beatles' manager, sold film footage of the group to the NBC network's late-night *Jack Paar Show*. It was shown to a large American audience on January 3. Stores all across the country offered Beatles wigs, dolls, rings, notebooks, tennis shoes, bubble gum, and bubble bath. Novelty records hit the airwaves with titles such as "Christmas With the Beatles," "My Boyfriend Got a Beatles Haircut," and "I Love Ringo." Still, America was where rock 'n' roll began, and many potential fans were skeptical.

On Friday, February 7, the band climbed aboard a Pan American airliner for the flight from London to New York. As they relaxed in their plush first-class seats, the Beatles got to know their fellow passengers. Instead of the usual transatlantic flyers, the seats were filled with businesspeople who wanted to make deals for endorsements or to manufacture Beatles trinkets. The quartet was met at New York's John F. Kennedy International Airport that afternoon by about four thousand young fans and enough burly police to keep the noisy crowd at a distance.

Everything was going according to plan, yet the Beatles, for all their popularity, were concerned. Paul McCartney voiced it best during their westward flight: "They've got their own groups," he said of United States music fans. "What are we going to give them that they don't already have?"[1] Because the young English musicians had heard of Carnegie Hall but not *The Ed Sullivan Show,* they were more worried about their stage performance in two weeks before a few thousand fans than the nationwide television exposure in two days in front of millions of viewers.

Ed Sullivan, the newspaper gossip columnist and host of his own top-rated weekly variety show, realized that the Beatles' appearance was almost coincidental. Sullivan had been in London's Heathrow Airport on Halloween in 1963 when John, Paul, George, and Ringo returned from a European concert. He saw the rockers being pursued by hundreds of crazed, clamoring teenagers and immediately wanted the four young men for his very popular Sunday-night show.

There was nothing automatic about this first American appearance. In fact, a brief tour of Paris a month earlier had been a fiasco. There was a brawl backstage, the Beatles were not given top billing, and they did not take the stage until after midnight. The French audience enjoyed the band's driving rock numbers but yawned whenever the quartet attempted a ballad. The Beatles had attracted little notice in Paris, though their records were selling all over western Europe. Would a prime-time television appearance in the United States succeed or fail?

On the evening of Sunday, February 9, American music buffs everywhere turned to their television sets.

The night was a cold and snowy one in Springfield, Ohio, for example. Inside a dormitory at Wittenberg University, students gathered around the big black-and-white television set in the lounge. These young adults had grown up with rock music, and they waited impatiently. Could the four musicians be as entertaining as the Isley Brothers from nearby Cincinnati? The voices of African-American musicians such as the Isleys tore into tunes like "Shout!," one of many songs capable of turning otherwise normal college crowds into dancing maniacs.

More than two thousand miles west, teenagers relaxed in front of a television in a family room in La Jolla, California. The West Coast was the home of the Beach Boys and surf music—who were the Beatles, anyway? In New York City's Peppermint Lounge, where Chubby Checker and the Twist had launched a major dance fad in the early 1960s, viewers also withheld judgment. And in Memphis, Tennessee, where black songs sung and played by white people originated rock 'n' roll, musicians set aside their instruments and turned to their screens.

John Lennon, Paul McCartney, George Harrison, and Ringo Starr—the Beatles—ran on stage amid nonstop screaming by the young, mostly female, audience. The girls cried, collapsed, and tore at the theater's seats as Lennon played rhythm guitar, McCartney played bass, Harrison played lead guitar, and

Starr beat on the drums. McCartney sang the lead on most songs, as he had done during dress rehearsal earlier that day. No one noticed that Harrison was suffering from the flu. The group began by singing "All My Loving," and most of the 728 persons in the theater wished the pleasant harmony would never end. So did much of the country.

McCartney, audiences noticed, was cute, Starr was fun, and Harrison appeared to be quiet and a very nice guy, despite his illness. Lennon remained a mystery. Lennon enjoyed shocking people by making clever remarks.[2] Tonight he behaved, dressed like the others in a dark, plain, tight-fitting suit. If his mind wandered, he may have been thinking about how different this life was from his younger days in the gritty English industrial city of Liverpool. Though he grew up in a pleasant, comfortable home, the riches the group's music would bring in were beyond his wildest dreams.

John Lennon was the only married Beatle at the time, so his thoughts might have drifted to his wife, Cynthia, and his year-old son, Julian. Lennon saw them infrequently due to the frantic pace of shows and rehearsals. Lennon's marriage was a fact manager Brian Epstein tried for some time to conceal—America's teenage girls were less likely to swoon over Lennon if they knew he had a wife and child awaiting him in England.

Lennon and the other band members put up with

Beatlemania. To them, it meant being cooped up in hotels or recording studios, never able to walk down the street without being chased by fans. Lennon accepted the craziness. Though his younger life was devoid of real hardship, Lennon always identified with the outcast, the underdog, the rebel, and the nonconformist.[3] He blended this outlook with incredible song-writing ability to become one of the world's best-known musicians, a musician who could truly be called an artist.

The Beatles' first live performance in the United States was seen by an astonishing 73.9 million viewers—the biggest audience in television history at the time.[4] Their light, sweet songs, written mostly by Lennon and McCartney, stuck in fans' memories. Not many in the audience stopped to wonder where the Beatles came from or how they had picked up on rock 'n' roll.

2

School Days

John Lennon was born at 6:30 P.M. on October 9, 1940, in Oxford Street Maternity Hospital, Liverpool, England. At the time, that was not news. Rather, headlines all across the country were telling of the Battle of Britain. German dictator Adolf Hitler's mighty military machine was attempting to soften up England with air raids prior to an invasion—in fact, bombs were dropped on Liverpool the night John Lennon was born. But a group of skilled British flyers was holding off the Germans in the air. Though Poland, Norway, Belgium, the Netherlands, and France had fallen to Hitler at the beginning of World War II, Great Britain would survive.

Among those involved in the war was Alfred (known as Alf or Freddy) Lennon, John's father. Of Irish ancestry, Alfred was a ship's steward based in Liverpool on England's northwest coast. He sailed the choppy, dangerous Atlantic on a variety of vessels before and during the war. Many of the ships were vulnerable to attacks by unseen U-boats, Germany's submarines. Julia Stanley, John's mother, was a Liverpool-area woman who became attracted to Freddy, a man who visited faraway places such as New York City. The two dated, got along, and were married three weeks before Christmas 1938.

Julia worked as a theater attendant. After the wedding, Alf sailed away on ships carrying soldiers and supplies to or from Africa, Canada, and elsewhere. Julia seldom saw him, and as the war broke out and continued, she failed to receive many letters or much money from her husband. In 1944, Julia met a British army officer while working as a waitress in a Liverpool restaurant. She and young John were living with Julia's father, and she was soon forced to tell her dad that she was pregnant and that the officer had disappeared. A daughter, Victoria Elizabeth, was born in 1945 and quickly adopted by a couple from Norway.[1]

Trying to recover from her unfortunate affair, Julia Lennon met and moved in with a hotel waiter named John Dykins. For Julia's older sister, Mimi Smith, that move was the last straw. Mimi confronted Julia in mid-1945, demanding that little John be turned over to her and her husband, who were without children, for a more stable home. Julia was unconvinced—until Mimi returned with a social worker. Together, they persuaded John's mother that the boy would be better off with her sister. So John joined Uncle George and Aunt Mimi in the Smith home at 251 Menlove Avenue, Woolton, a middle-class suburb of Liverpool.

Julia had christened her son John Winston Lennon, probably because she admired Winston Churchill. The wartime prime minister was the symbol of a defiant, eventually victorious, Britain. By the time John entered primary school in September 1945, the war was over, Churchill was no longer prime minister, and England was a very different place. Everyday British residents were determined to have more of a say in the way their lives and government were run.

John's Uncle George worked at a dairy farm begun by his great-grandfather, who started with only a single cow. The farm had grown over the years. Though she had worked earlier as a nurse, Aunt Mimi stayed at home with John. He had his own room and showed an early preference for books over toys. Postwar Britain was a hard place in which to live—many of the ancient cities had been bombed into rubble by the Germans, and there were quotas (called rationing) on everything from chocolate to gasoline. Liverpool, with its miles of docks along the Mersey River, had played a vital part in the war effort, but its industries were old, and there were many more people than jobs.

In the nineteenth century, the city of more than half

a million, along with the surrounding county of Merseyside, had attracted thousands of people from Ireland desperate for work. Liverpool had a certain worldliness—sailors returned with exotic foreign goods and even more exotic stories. Residents turned to actors and artists and musicians for amusement after long days of hard work. Though it would be several years before John Lennon realized it, this old city was the perfect spot for a person such as him to grow up.

For a while, it appeared that Lennon might grow up elsewhere. Alf Lennon turned up suddenly in Liverpool in the summer of 1946 and persuaded Aunt Mimi to let him take John to the beach for the day. John's father was planning a new life with his son by migrating to faraway New Zealand.[2] When the two did not return after several days, Mimi alerted Julia, John's mother. Julia had been in contact with her son all along, and John liked the idea of having both his aunt and his mother to look out for him.[3] Julia found Alf and John in a seaside boarding house.

Alf told his son that he had to choose between his two parents.[4] Having enjoyed the holiday spent by the sea, with his father buying him treats, John tearfully decided to remain with his dad.[5] Julia tried to convince John otherwise, but her pleas were interrupted by John's father, who pointed out that the boy had made his choice. Julia had gone only a short distance when John caught up with her, tears streaming down his face. Julia returned John to Uncle George and Aunt Mimi's comfortable home, and Alf Lennon was not seen again for many years.

John was enrolled by his aunt in Dovedale Road Primary School shortly before his fifth birthday. Uncle George had already taught John to read—he would pull the boy onto his lap every evening, and the two went through the newspaper page by page, figuring out each word in the headlines. When the school's headmaster told Mimi that John was "[as] sharp as a needle," she was not surprised.[6] John learned to express himself early, not only by studying printed words but spoken words, as well.

Commercial radio was enormously popular at the time, delivering drama, comedy, music, advice, and news to millions of British homes. John loved mysteries, sitting on the edge of his bed as an English secret agent foiled plans by enemy governments or ferreted out spies from within. He also was addicted to comedies such as *The Goon Show,* a weekly program filled with puns, impossible accents, one-line jokes, and other silliness. He may have practiced reading with his uncle, but he practiced dopey comedy with his patient aunt.

Not much astonished Aunt Mimi. She was not surprised, for example, when the innocent-appearing little boy, who hiked off to the school on Penny Lane every day in a black blazer, grey shorts, white shirt, and tie, got into trouble with his teachers. John was on the edge of trouble virtually from the start of his school days. While other boys slid down an icy hill, kicked a football, or played marbles, John led an unruly pack of boys who could always be found by following their rude and noisy laughter. The Lennon mob irked most teachers and a number of fellow students.[7]

John told an interviewer years later that he knew he was different from others, even as a child. He also admitted that Aunt Mimi kept him well fed and well dressed, though he was not always well mannered. He was, he recalled, "a nice lower-middle-class English boy."[8]

Aunt Mimi's philosophy about raising John was simple. She made him obey her rules at home but decided enforcement was not her job when he was elsewhere. When the school's headmaster (principal) asked what should be done with the child she was raising, Aunt Mimi demanded to know when the authorities were going to make the boy behave in school! Occasionally, John did get involved in his work. He read almost anything, and he spent a lot of time on his art-class drawings. Artistic ability and flashes of talent in most other classes except math may have saved the future star from worse things than an occasional spanking. Lennon easily passed the nationwide test that allowed him to continue past elementary school.

The summer he was fourteen, another aunt took him on vacation in Scotland. When John returned, Aunt

Mimi told him that Uncle George had died of a hemorrhage. Uncle George was never ill, and he did not become excited by raising his voice to the boy. The kindly uncle had hauled John to the dairy, where they poked among the cattle, or had taken him along on shopping trips, past places with names like Strawberry Field, spending generously. In his grief, John became better friends with his mother, the two young girls she had borne with John Dykins, and Dykins himself. Despite her impulsive ways, John grew to like Julia.[9] Like her son, she did not think much of authority.

Those who ran Quarry Bank School, where John attended high school, saw immediately in 1952 that young Lennon would be a problem. John launched his attack in several ways: He hated sports, preferring to make fun of overweight classmates rather than trying to beat them in cross-country runs. He drew merciless cartoons of the teachers, he smoked, he swore, he fought, he stole, and he looked a mess despite leaving Aunt Mimi's house squeaky clean every morning. She bought him glasses, which he needed, thinking better vision would mean better grades. Such was not the case—John hated being seen wearing spectacles. One of several school reports told Aunt Mimi he was "on the road to failure."[10]

The thing John found most interesting in his teenage life proved to be a radio station that was not only unconventional but very difficult to find or hear. Radio

Luxembourg was a real contrast to the stodgy format on the various British Broadcasting Corporation (BBC) stations at the time. The Luxembourgers played American jazz, blues, country, and a new kind of hybrid music with an incessant beat—rock and roll. John and teenagers all over England huddled around their radios late at night to hear songs by Chuck Berry, Bill Haley, Screamin' Jay Hawkins, and others. The music gave them something to share. That something, enhanced by American films, became a lifestyle.

Being a teenage rebel in England at the time required that John become a Teddy Boy. Such kids were called juvenile delinquents or hoodlums in the United States, where they wore T-shirts, jeans, and leather jackets. But in Great Britain, teenage boys put on black cloth jackets with velvet collars, flashy shirts, string ties, tight black "stovepipe" pants, socks that may have been shocking pink, and various kinds of thick-soled shoes. The fad was in full bloom in 1955, the year an American movie, *Rock Around the Clock*, was shown in England. Though it was little more than a series of musical performances strung together on film, the film took the island nation's teenagers by storm.

Bill Haley and the Comets performed the song for which the movie was named. Teddy Boys responded by ripping theater seats, screaming, fighting, and other forms of misbehavior. The boys—and their girlfriends— began buying records by the millions. Numerous British musicians saw that rock was the future and started playing it in earnest. Among the most successful was Lonnie Donegan, a pioneer of the skiffle band. Skiffle meant taking an American rock, country, or blues tune and bending words and music rapidly around so that it was more to the tastes of British listeners.

John Lennon heard and saw what was going on. He could have remained one of the millions of boys who bought records, listened to the radio, and ran rock and roll around in his head. Instead, he decided to make his own kind of music.[11]

3

Making Music

The nearsighted teenager leaned into the bedroom mirror as he worked on the jellyroll he called his hair. The front of the boy's auburn locks pointed like the tip of a canoe toward the glass. He combed the sides past his ears and smoothed his wispy sideburns. Then, with every greasy, shiny tuft in place, John Lennon began to quake, strut, wiggle, and sing, just like his idol, Elvis Presley.

"I had no idea about doing music as a way of life until rock 'n' roll hit me," John would remember. "It wasn't until 'Heartbreak Hotel' [by Elvis Presley] that I really got into it."[1]

Elvis reached Great Britain in about 1957 on one of the late-night shows from Radio Luxembourg with his first international hit, "Heartbreak Hotel." Performances on television and in the movies followed. John was immediately entranced—as were his friends and millions of English teenagers.[2] Skiffle music was all right, but Elvis was a whole other scene. He was, one writer pointed out, almost beyond imitation. Just as John became convinced that no one could affect him like Elvis, someone played Little Richard's hit single, "Long Tall Sally/Slippin' and Slidin'," and the future Beatle was overwhelmed.[3] Where had this music been all his life?

John began to pester Aunt Mimi for a guitar. While he worked on her, he sent away for an inexpensive, mail-order model. Though it did not have metal strings or even a very good sound, John strummed the crude acoustic instrument for hours. Aunt Mimi thought Elvis Presley was a marginal talent at best, so she banished John and his guitar to the glassed-in porch. Her nephew virtually disappeared from every other room in the house, whanging away on the guitar from the time he got home from school until bedtime, with only a few minutes out to bolt down his evening meal.

The young suburbanite hauled his instrument to his mother's place, where she showed him how to tune the guitar to complement the banjo she sometimes played. Julia was a good musician, and so, for that matter, was John. He had earlier played the accordion and had fooled around with a small instrument that would be revived by rock and rollers: the harmonica. At the same time, he got to know other musicians his age at school and railed at his friends until they, too, acquired instruments. Dressed in tight-fitting black jeans, the members of John's teenage band called themselves the Black Jacks.

Their first gig was not exactly Lincoln Center. The Black Jacks stood on the back of a truck during a neighborhood block party and attempted to play the few tunes they knew. Several other jobs quickly followed, primarily because most other musical groups demanded money and John felt the opportunity to play was reward enough. Mimi herself saw a performance by the struggling teenage group one afternoon at a church garden party. John, always a willing lead singer, overcame his aunt's scrutiny to belt out a number of Presley and other tunes. Aunt Mimi was not the only important person in the audience. A fifteen-year-old guitar player from a musical family witnessed the performance and became interested. The date was July 6, 1957, and the young musician was named James Paul McCartney.

Through a mutual friend who was a member of John's band, Lennon and McCartney met after the performance. Paul, always quick to praise, said he thought the band had a good sound. Then the left-handed player picked up his guitar and dazzled the group, not only playing chords they did not know existed but singing several American rock and roll tunes. He knew the words, and his voice was pleasant. He even showed the other boys how to tune a guitar. John wanted Paul, who had received some formal musical education, in the band. "Paul taught me how to play the guitar proper . . ."[4] John would later admit.

When John was not playing or doing as little as possible at school, he went to the movies. He picked up a number of cues from James Dean, the melancholy actor who played a troubled teenager in *Rebel Without a Cause*, and Marlon Brando, who portrayed a motorcycle gangster in *The Wild One*. He also studied great and one-shot American rockers who appeared in movies with titles like *The Girl Can't Help It* and *Jukebox Saturday Night*. The music movies were created to let young rock fans see the people they had only heard. Although John did not have the money to attend live performances, United States stars began including Great Britain in their tours. Musicians ranged from a veteran Chicago blues rocker named Bo Diddley to upstart Californians such as Eddie Cochran and Gene Vincent. John knew their songs by heart.

For every song he learned, he seemed to forget a part of his schooling. Aunt Mimi was disappointed but hardly surprised when John flunked a national test that might have allowed him to enter a major university following high school. Lennon failed each part of the exam by a point or so, indicating a lack of interest rather than lack of ability. His final day at Quarry Bank School took place only a short time after meeting Paul

McCartney. The departure was ironic because his musical group had only recently changed its name to the Quarry Men.

John recovered from academic failure by gathering his drawings—including nasty sketches of several teachers—and presenting himself to the admissions office of the Liverpool College of Art. He was often serious about drawing, and his samples helped him gain admission. School began in September—right around the corner from the Institute, where several Quarry Men, including Paul McCartney, were in high school. One of Paul's classmates also would go on to fame. The third and youngest Beatle, George Harrison, was already into guitar music and Teddy Boy attire when Lennon shifted from high school in the suburbs to art college in a gritty old section of downtown Liverpool.

Later, John remembered his relationship with George, who idolized him: "he was like a disciple of mine when we started . . ."[5] George was several years younger than John, who was enrolled in art college while George was barely out of grammar school.

John had become much closer to his mother at about the same time. He sometimes moved in with her, John Dykins, and the couple's two daughters for several days at a time. In fact, Lennon and Dykins were awaiting Julia on the fateful night of July 15, 1958. John's mother had been visiting Aunt Mimi, and she left her sister's home shortly before 10 P.M. The street there was divided by an old trolley line covered in hedge. Julia stepped through an opening in the vegetation, intending to catch a bus. She was hit by a car driven by an off-duty policeman. Though an ambulance was quickly called, Julia Lennon died before she reached the hospital.

"I lost her twice," John would later confess. "Once as a five year old when I moved in with my auntie, once again when she died. It just absolutely made me *very, very* bitter."[6]

John managed to hold on in his various art classes, and one of his artsy new friends became a source of comfort. This young man with talent to spare was named Stuart Sutcliffe. He and John may have hit it off so readily because they were complete opposites. Stuart was outwardly gentle and tough as nails inside. Unlike John, Sutcliffe was serious—he never made fun of anyone or caused any kind of ruckus. Yet he had a tremendous inner drive and often had blinding headaches as he concentrated ferociously on his artwork. John, on the other hand, created a hide of armor that hid an inner person with a great deal of feeling.[7] Somehow, the two fed off each other and became great friends. Though Stuart had little musical ability, John recruited him for the band.

Like many reluctant students, the lunch period was John's favorite time of the day. Each day he would run off to a nearby diner for a big, carryout helping of greasy, deep-fried potatoes, then retrieve Paul McCartney and

George Harrison from their high school nearby. The trio and others would play their guitars and sing in the art-college lunchroom as an audience with a number of lovely female students ate and listened. The girls were of two minds about John—most found his Teddy Boy looks and his wicked sense of humor frightening. Yet there were others who felt Lennon was almost hypnotic. Among them was a heartbreakingly good-looking student by the name of Cynthia Powell.

Described by a classmate as resembling French movie star Brigitte Bardot, Cynthia was a year older than John. Unlike the rude and boisterous entertainer, she was quiet and from a small town some distance from Liverpool. Lennon was strongly attracted to Cynthia, but he hung around with several other girls while trying to find out more about her.[8] About the only thing they shared was a one-parent home—Cynthia's father, a sales representative, had died several years earlier. Despite his lack of polish, John sang Buddy Holly songs aimed at Cynthia's heart during his lunchtime performances. The tunes must have worked, because the two soon became inseparable.

Despite the fact that "he frightened me to death," Cynthia showed up whenever John and the band played.[9] She gave John change so that he could buy guitar strings, she dyed her hair blonde to please him, and she bought tight-fitting bohemian clothing that showed off her figure. John shed some of the Teddy Boy look for clothing that made him resemble a beatnik—a shabby, starving artist. Black jacket, black turtleneck sweater, black pants—the attire often smelled strongly of cigarette smoke and potatoes fried in grease, two of Lennon's addictions. John, Cynthia, and others hung out in several coffeehouses, though they continued to show up more or less regularly for art class. They always turned up for a performance, though not always on time.

The boys played in dark basement clubs with names like the Casbah and Jacaranda. They earned less than $10 per date apiece, though Allan Williams, who owned the Jacaranda, helped point them in the direction of stardom. He mentioned that a London promoter would be holding auditions in Liverpool soon and that the group might want to perform. Williams and John argued over a new name for the band, and Lennon picked the Beetles. He felt it was akin to Buddy Holly's backup group, the Crickets, and it suggested the band had a strong beat, which it certainly did. At Williams's urging, John settled on the Silver Beetles, and the band practiced frantically.

Liverpool was a city of bands, and dozens of talented musical groups showed up to audition. Times were hard—the promoter's foremost interest was in a band that would work cheaply. All of the groups were willing, and all were handsomely attired in suits—except the Silver Beetles. They combined turtleneck sweaters, tight jeans, and tennis shoes with high volume and rowdy behavior to win the mind, if not the heart, of the promoter. The Silver Beetles were hired for a two-week tour of Scotland as the backup band for a singer named Johnny Gentle. Though band members each made only a bit over $50 a week on the tour, which they spent on hotels and food, John returned home not wanting to do anything else.[10]

John and Paul in particular practiced ceaselessly. Paul's father did not think much of Lennon, so the boys could only make music in the McCartney home during the day, when Mr. McCartney was working. They also used the home of John Dykins, and they played in Stuart Sutcliffe's shabby little apartment. Paul had an eye for detail, and John had a sixth sense about rock music. They decided, during one of many sessions, that all of their future songs would carry the "Lennon-McCartney" writing label. George Harrison was not yet a writer, and Stuart was no musician. Neither was as dependent as John was on Paul and vice-versa.[11]

The Beatles, as they now called themselves, settled back into the routine of playing for tough people in bad parts of town. John decided in July 1960 not to return to the Liverpool College of Art and to focus instead on his music. He was terribly impressed—perhaps even a bit jealous—that Paul had written a number of songs, and he wanted to concentrate on turning his thoughts and feelings into music.[12] First he had to deal with the fact that the drummer, Tommy Moore, had run out of patience and quit the band. With four guitars and no one on drums, the group's future looked grim.

Once again, Allan Williams came to their rescue. In exchange for painting one of Williams's apartments, the Beatles were booked into a club in Hamburg, Germany, a northern port very similar to Liverpool. Looking around before they left, the boys learned that Mona Best, owner of the Casbah coffeehouse, had a son who played drums. Even better, son Peter's band had just broken up, and he hoped to join another bunch of Liverpool rockers. Best's abilities were limited, but John, Paul, George, and Stuart Sutcliffe could ill afford to be particular. The five set off for the ferry boat to Germany in Allan Williams's minibus, which groaned under the weight of passengers, instruments, amplifiers, suitcases, and more. What would the gig at the Indra Club in Hamburg bring?

4

The Beatles
Come Together

Sailors and other people went looking for a good time in the meanest part of Hamburg, Germany. There were hundreds of bars and clubs, and vice of all kinds flourished. To lure big spenders, club owners hired entertainment—strippers in some places, bands in others. Some bands could pull people in off the sidewalk. The Beatles, playing every American song they had ever learned, certainly were one such band.

The songs of the Everly Brothers, Chuck Berry, Elvis Presley, and Little Richard changed the Indra Club from a small and filthy place with a few quiet drinkers to a small and filthy place bulging with people of all nationalities who felt the urge to boogie. The Beatles were paid less than $50 apiece weekly to play music every night from 7 P.M. to 3 A.M. They usually performed six forty-five-minute sets, two or three times as much music as bands play in any given evening. The club's owner provided them with a dingy sleeping room behind a movie screen in a nearby theater he owned. If the Beatles overslept, they risked being awakened by the sounds of a matinee!

Lennon thrived on the atmosphere. He leapt about on the cramped little stage, screaming lyrics and muttering insults at the audience under his breath. As the music built each evening and the crowd became virtually as loud as the instruments, no one heard Lennon call the audience Nazis, or remind them their tanks were double parked![1] For all its squalor, Hamburg made the band tougher. Not many groups could play for hours without repeating songs. Nor could they crank up the volume and speed as the audience and its excitement grew. But the Beatles certainly could.

Several important things happened in Hamburg during their stay from August to December 1960. The group soon moved to a bigger club, the Kaiserkeller, alternating play for eight hours each night with another Liverpool group, Rory and the Hurricanes. The two bands hung around together, seeking out places where they could eat fish and chips and other English food and talk about music. The drummer for the Hurricanes was Richard Starkey, who also went by the name of Ringo Starr. Stuart Sutcliffe had met a pretty German girl and, because he was an artist rather than a musician, lost interest in the Beatles. He moved in with his new girlfriend and her mother.

Their commitment to rock and roll was the Beatles' undoing in Germany. In violation of the band's contract, they played in a jam session with another group in a rival nightclub. The Kaiserkeller's owner took revenge by turning George Harrison in because he was a foreign minor, who therefore was working illegally. The authorities sent Harrison back to England on the first available plane. At about the same time, McCartney and Best accidentally started the curtains on fire in their grimy theater apartment. The band got back to England any way it could, with Lennon traveling alone on a train most of the way. Once again, everyone was broke, and Lennon was discouraged.[2]

Yet the driving music they had developed in Hamburg made the Beatles a hit in Liverpool. They were hired to play at a basement club called the Cavern. Each day at lunch the band played two forty-five-minute sets. For this, Lennon earned about $75 a week, better than usual but not enough to thrive. Throughout 1961, they played where they could, including Hamburg, where they returned as soon as George turned eighteen. Stuart Sutcliffe stayed in Germany, so the Beatles were once again a quintet. The only good thing that could be said about this period was that the band got into a recording studio. They backed up a popular British singer named Tony Sheridan on "My Bonnie Lies Over the Ocean" and "When the Saints Go Marching In." Nowhere on the record label were the Beatles mentioned.

Lennon and McCartney believed their careers were going nowhere.[3] That fall, they canceled their club dates and, despite a lack of money, went to Paris. They returned with even less money two weeks later. To make ends meet, they found Harrison and Best and signed on once again to play in Liverpool's clubs. Between the city's many musicians and the growing rock audience, the guys were gaining a following. One of their fans was an intelligent young man whose parents owned a furniture store. He did not mind selling furniture, but he convinced his folks that the music business was a better bet. With parental assistance, Brian Epstein opened two record shops that were highly successful.

Epstein, looking out of place in his suit in the Cavern, found the Beatles crude but hypnotic. "I had never seen anything like the Beatles on any stage. . . . They turned their backs on the audience and shouted at them and laughed at private jokes."[4]

Mustering his courage—he was quiet and rather shy—Epstein hauled the four back to his plush office in December 1961 and offered to manage them. Puzzled but impressed by Epstein's nice clothes, careful manners, and ritzy furniture, the Beatles nodded. The nods may have drawn Epstein's eyes toward their moppy haircuts, one of their souvenirs of Hamburg. Given them a few months earlier by Stuart Sutcliffe's girlfriend, the hair styles would become one of their trademarks.

The new manager worked hard to keep the band in line. To make sure the Beatles showed up on time for their shows, he drove from house to house, picking them up. He nagged at them about the way they were dressed, pointing out that record-company executives might not have much patience for any group that looked like they did. Slowly, he eased them into dark suits that were virtually free of any kind of ornamentation. Best of all, he quickly got them an audition with Decca Records in London. The band did a lackluster job, primarily because Epstein talked them into singing old standard tunes rather than rock and roll. The manager insisted that Lennon, who had the best voice, sing at least half of the songs. Epstein realized early that John Lennon had mysterious drawing power.[5]

Cynthia Powell, Lennon's longtime girlfriend, certainly found him magnetic. She worried about the clusters of schoolgirls and secretaries who spent their lunch hours in the Cavern. Lennon began writing a column for a local music newspaper weekly, and that earned him even more fans. He not only told readers how the Beatles came to be, he amused them with sly wordplay, cartoons, and poems. It was a mark of Brian Epstein's effect on Lennon that the rocker demanded back from the newspaper some of his nastier poems, before they were printed. He was convinced by the

An early 1960s photo of the Beatles. From left: John Lennon, George Harrison, Paul McCartney, and Peter Best.

Beatles' manager that dirty words no longer fit the group's image.

Described by Lennon's Aunt Mimi as "a restless soul just like John," Epstein began the long uphill battle to find the Beatles a recording contract.[6] Meanwhile, the Beatles shuttled back and forth between Liverpool and Hamburg. One such trip began on April 10, 1962, when Stuart Sutcliffe's girlfriend, Astrid Kircherr, met them at the airport in Germany. Lennon could tell something was wrong from a distance.

"What's the matter?" he asked.

"Stuart died, John," Kircherr said. "He's gone."

Lennon's reaction would add to the legend that he was the "hard man" of the Beatles. Depending on which book is quoted, Lennon laughed, cried, or became hysterical.[7] Because Kircherr saw that Lennon was making a scene at the airport to conceal his pain, she said nothing. She knew that Lennon and Sutcliffe had exchanged many letters, telling each other about their girlfriends, their hopes, their dreams. Sutcliffe had suffered for several years from terrible headaches, but many people believed it had something to do with his artistic intensity. In fact, he died of a cerebral hemorrhage—a stroke. "How John got over that period I'll never know," Astrid noted.[8]

Lennon and the Beatles played on and on. Hamburg's plush Star Club was their showplace this time, and it was a large step up from the dismal and dirty places they had played earlier. The group lived in an apartment above the club, earning the huge sum of $150 apiece each week and behaving as most young men would at that stage of their lives. They had lots of parties, and there was a constant flow of humanity in and out of their living quarters. McCartney says of that period, "We were all just normal human beings."[9] Happily, McCartney and Lennon continued to write songs. Lennon's strength appeared to be in taking the skeleton of a song and fleshing it out, running with what had only been a phrase or a few bars of music.

Several events would break up the shuttling between Liverpool and Hamburg in 1962. After several unsuccessful tries, the Beatles landed themselves a recording contract. The four signed with Parlophone, a small label within a much larger company called EMI. The agreement was signed on May 9 and was followed less than a month later by a similar pact with EMI. The first recording session took place on June 6 in recording studios on Abbey Road in London. By this time, Peter Best had left as the group's drummer and Ringo Starr had signed on. Starr, Lennon noted later, was pleasant and "a damn good drummer."[10]

The Beatles, as the world would know them, finally were together. Initially, Lennon clearly was the group's leader. "I was . . . about a half a niche higher-class than Paul, George, and Ringo, who lived in

John Lennon and Cynthia Powell were married on August 23, 1962.

government-subsidized houses. . . . Ringo was the only real city kid."[11]

The quartet could almost smell success that summer, as a London-based television film crew recorded their act at the Cavern. The day after being filmed, on August 23, 1962, John Lennon married Cynthia Powell, who was pregnant. She was almost twenty-three years old, and Lennon was almost twenty-two. "We were both kids basically," Cynthia later recalled.[12] There was never any question whether the two should marry—Lennon clearly wanted to do the right thing. As for his new wife, she pointed out that "I didn't marry John for his money. He didn't have any."[13] Happily, after years of scraping along, that was about to change.

5

Beatlemania

In 1962, the Beatles were on the brink of success. Their breakthrough came in 1963, following hundreds of appearances in Liverpool, Hamburg, and many places in between. Compared to the Beatles, fame came to Elvis Presley almost overnight. The teenage truck driver made a demo record for his mother one day and was approached by the owner of a record company virtually the next. The Beatles suffered a number of setbacks but kept playing, confident of their ability not only to perform but to combine words and music in original ways.

"Love Me Do," the Beatles' first single, was recorded in September 1962 and released one month later. It entered Britain's most important list of hit records at the end of October and enjoyed considerable air play. To make the song distinctive, Lennon had reached into his musical past, punctuating the song with a brief but distinct harmonica solo. With each appearance, the crowds appeared to be more uncontrollably attracted to the music and the group that made it.

"Please Please Me," a song written by Lennon, was released on January 12, 1963. The quartet sang it on *Thank Your Lucky Stars*, a nationwide television show with a studio audience made up primarily of rabid Liverpool fans. The Liverpudlians made an incredible noise, probably convincing the television audience that this was how they should act whenever a Beatles song was performed. By March 1, "Please Please Me" was Britain's best-selling record.

Britain's *Daily Mirror* newspaper coined the term "Beatlemania" in its November 2, 1963, edition. Given what was happening, Beatlemania was almost an understatement. "Beatle leader John Lennon, 23, bawled for quiet," the paper reported from a Beatles concert in a London suburb. "It just brought more squeals."[1] The *Daily Mirror* noted that the quartet had just "swept Sweden" and was back in England for a series of appearances.

"As Lennon and his fellow Beatles . . . struggled manfully on, girls left their seats and rushed to the stage."[2] Such a performance—by audiences—would be repeated wherever the group performed. Wire-service photos in the United States and from the Philippines to

Scandinavia would show police attempting to hold back walls of young girls exhibiting the kind of behavior not seen since their older sisters tried to storm the stage as Elvis Presley sang and shook. Beatlemaniacs in America, anyway, were Baby Boomers in their early teens, and there were a great many of them. Lennon once looked over the sea of fans and lunging reporters and announced that the group would make no further unscheduled appearances during their tours. The more isolated the four became, the more young fans desperately tried to reach them.

Since the teenagers had lots of little brothers and sisters too young to see the Beatles in person, Beatles baubles and trinkets were cranked out in staggering numbers just for them. There was Beatles bubble bath courtesy of Colgate, The Beatles "Flip Your Wig" board game from Milton Bradley, and a complete line of official Beatles jewelry. For every legitimate souvenir or product, there were dozens of badly made pieces of junk, including pennants, pins, hats, bumper stickers, and fan-club membership cards. Today, both the authorized and unauthorized items are worth hundreds of dollars in good condition. A cardboard record-shop display for the *Yellow Submarine* album, for example, is now worth $1,800 in good condition!

The skyrocketing popularity of her husband was of little consolation to Cynthia Lennon. She realized the need to keep their marriage private, but there were many other things on her mind. First, she nearly miscarried her baby soon after the wedding in the early fall of 1962. Aunt Mimi forgave John and Cynthia their sudden marriage, inviting the new Mrs. Lennon to live with her while her husband toured with the band. Second, an increasing number of music fans showed up at Aunt Mimi's house, where Cynthia told them she was John's girlfriend. She did not reveal her marriage, claiming that her billowy clothing was what artists put on for a day of painting![3]

Lennon found that playing every day had its down side. Increasingly cooped up in buses and hotel rooms as their fame spread, the Beatles saw countryside, towns, and cities only from behind thick windows. They used the time to choreograph their songs, to write new songs, and to practice new melodies. A driver for the group recalls Lennon in particular: "I remember him telling me that he could get ideas for his songs from reading. . . . He always had books or magazines or newspapers when he was on the coach for hours on end."[4]

If McCartney and Harrison were talented musicians, and if McCartney was emerging as the group's spokesperson, Lennon always had the last word. McCartney constantly thought up new things to do, on stage and off, but he ran them past Lennon before going any further. If Lennon said no, then the idea was dismissed. In news conferences, where McCartney spoke more and more for the group, Lennon played the heavy—he injected sarcasm or black humor that increased his reputation as the Beatles' tough guy. He also was the least satisfied of the group, finding ways afterward to improve even the liveliest performance.[5]

To while away idle time, Lennon took turns teasing everyone. Eyeing his distinctive haircut in a dressing-room mirror, he announced to the other three that he had terrible dandruff and that he would soon cut all of his hair off! He signed autographs mechanically, often scribbling his name on a program or paper while watching television. Yet behind his tough image, he was thinking about the future. After getting to know Mick Jagger, he told the lead singer of the Rolling Stones that "I didn't want to be fiddling round the world singing 'Please Please Me' when I'm thirty."[6]

The performer's patience was quickly tested. He tired of meeting public officials as true fans were kept away and cameras clicked. Lennon also resented police and promoters. "I bet every bloody policeman's daughter in Britain's got an autograph," he said. "Half of them aren't our fans. It's unfair on the kids who really want them."[7]

With outbursts like that, no wonder McCartney told him, "You're bad for my image!"[8]

Besides being outspoken, Lennon could be cruel. Brian Epstein, the Beatles' efficient and conscientious manager, often was belittled by Lennon. Lennon made disparaging, anti-Semitic remarks about Epstein's Jewish

John Lennon (foreground) and Paul McCartney tune their guitars prior to a performance in England in 1963. The police in the background were assigned to keep fans from throwing themselves at the stage.

heritage and other aspects of his character. Ironically, Epstein continued to like and admire the most outspoken, least considerate member of the quartet.[9]

Lennon had other things on his mind. Cynthia delivered a son, John Charles Julian, on April 8, 1963, and her musician husband was unable to see the child for three days due to his hectic schedule. The Beatles had just stormed across Britain with American singers Chris Montez and Tommy Roe, and they were about to do so again with United States legend Roy Orbison and fellow Liverpool residents Gerry and the Pacemakers. Lennon managed to return to Liverpool to gaze on mother and child, who were doing well enough.

Unfortunately, Lennon was not always able to control his drinking. Whenever the Beatles were playing in London, Lennon could be found late at night at his favorite bar, the Ad Lib Club. A haunt of celebrities, Lennon would show up there after a performance, order Scotch and Coca-Cola, smoke heavily, and drink until he became annoying. It was the drunken Lennon's habit to collar someone—it could be anyone—and force his opinion on that person in an incessant, braying voice. He also voiced strong, usually negative, opinions of various rock groups, at times in front of members of such groups.[10]

Perhaps it was fortunate that Epstein helped arrange for their first American visit early in 1964. Lennon's prickliness concerning Beatlemania did not make even his closest friends comfortable. He hated the fact that screams from the audience drowned out perfectly good songs, and he frequently ended a tune either by pantomiming the words or by shouting an obscenity only Harrison, McCartney, or Starr might hear. In his defense, he believed fans were losing sight of the fact that the Beatles were good writers and musicians. Instead, Lennon saw the four increasingly as performers, not much different from circus animals, moving from town to town doing pathetic tricks.[11]

6

Money and Fame

Suddenly, the Beatles were rich. Very, very rich.

Though they were too busy making appearances to do much else, the group's bank accounts were swelling with royalties, the payments that come from writing songs and from other kinds of art. The trouble, of course, was that the nonstop schedule Epstein devised prevented them from enjoying the tons and tons of cash. Harrison, McCartney, and Starr all bought expensive movie cameras and shot film wherever they went, aiming lenses out of car windows, motels, and airplanes. Lennon contented himself with buying all the available books and magazines he could find while on tour.

Back in the United Kingdom, Lennon was as extravagant as anyone. On a return trip to Liverpool, Lennon saw that fans were huddled outside the house

The Beatles arrived in America in 1964. Waving, from left, are John Lennon, Paul McCartney, George Harrison, and Ringo Starr. Several thousand curious New Yorkers turned out in February cold at Kennedy Airport to see the quartet.

where he had grown up. He offered to buy Aunt Mimi a house wherever she might like to live, and Aunt Mimi mentioned Bournemouth, a seaside resort. Aunt Mimi and John climbed into his new, chauffeur-driven Rolls-Royce and found an attractive home for the widow in Bournemouth that looked out over the ocean. Aunt Mimi sold her famous home in the Liverpool suburb of Woolton and quietly moved.

Though Liverpool had spawned a number of rock and pop musicians, it still was not the recording center that London was. So John and Cynthia Lennon, during a rare day or two off in the summer of 1964, went shopping for a home. They found a large suburban dwelling in Weybridge, Surrey, in an area nicknamed "the stockbroker belt" for the number of spacious, expensive mansions. Shortly before departing Liverpool for the last time as residents, Lennon and fellow Beatles took part in a reception in their honor. More than one hundred thousand Liverpudlians lined the highway from the airport into the city. The quartet acted graciously in front of longtime fans.

Once in their new home in London, John, Cynthia, and little Julian, as he was called, lived with great extravagance. So did Harrison, McCartney, and Starr, who also purchased big suburban homes. None of the Beatles could safely be seen on the street anymore, so Epstein sometimes arranged for stores to close and for the musicians to be admitted so they could pick out whatever they liked. Harrod's, a famous department store, shut its doors one day late in 1964 so that the Beatles could complete their Christmas shopping. Lennon once paid a private visit to an exclusive shop, leaving a few minutes after having spent nearly $150,000.

He quickly decorated his new home in crazy colors and lined it with dozens of trinkets and mementoes. They included:

- A television set in virtually every room. Lennon enjoyed having each television on but with the sound turned off.

- At least a dozen guitars, including his first Rickenbacker model. The battered instrument had been purchased in Germany during one of the first Hamburg tours several years earlier.

- Three cars. Besides the Rolls-Royce with its chauffeur, there was a subcompact Mini-Cooper and an Italian Ferrari. Lennon admitted he was a terrible driver, but he did pass the test to obtain a license.

- A swimming pool. Lennon had the pool installed after he moved in, telling friends that all big houses should have pools, even in the frequently cloudy, damp English weather.

- A huge record collection. Besides all of the usual rock and roll classics, Lennon enjoyed listening to Indian and classical music, in particular.

- Two pictures drawn by his old friend, Stuart Sutcliffe, plus various drawings that Lennon dashed off and liked well enough to at least leave lying around.

- Mechanical toys for adults, from a juke box to a pinball machine to a box on the mantle that did nothing but flash a red light in an unpredictable pattern.

Cynthia and Julian were the only ones who spent enough time in the suburban estate to enjoy it. Shortly after returning from the Beatles' first tour of the United States in 1964, the four began to work on their first movie, *A Hard Day's Night*. Lennon's first book, *In His Own Write*, was published. Critics said the movie, which they very much liked, reminded them of a Marx brothers comedy. The action was frantic and constant as one Beatle ran out one door while a second Beatle ran in the other. The producer got the idea for perpetual action after taking a cross-London cab ride with the band and watching as they ordered the vehicle to stop for newspapers, then cigarettes, then a snack, and so on.

A Hard Day's Night was cleverly written. The creators knew that people wanted to watch the Beatles act like musicians on stage and like themselves off. The plot was almost nonexistent but centered around character actor Wilfrid Brambell, who played

John Lennon (right) sings lead vocals and plays harmony while Paul McCartney (left) plays bass and George Harrison, next to Paul, plays the melody. Lennon admitted that he was not a great guitarist, but his presence on the stage was said to be magnetic. This performance was part of the movie *A Hard Day's Night*.

John Lennon (right) and the other Beatles get their hair styled on the set of *A Hard Day's Night,* the group's first movie, shot in 1964.

McCartney's grandfather. The elderly gentleman watches as the Beatles are mobbed whenever they step out into any street. Much of the movie is taken up with the Fab Four running successfully away from a mob of fans. The band had no control over the script but did perform the title song and others with their usual showmanship and musical ability. Filmed for just over $500,000, the picture made millions.

In His Own Write also was a marked success. It contained nothing more than familiar stories on which Lennon had put strange, sometimes funny spins. He used crazy spellings and puns to produce parodies of familiar people and events. The book sold about one hundred thousand copies during its first printing. Lennon reluctantly volunteered himself for autograph parties in connection with the release of *In His Own Write*. Veterans of Liverpool music news found many of Lennon's most familiar themes and phrases between the covers.

Lennon had a way with words, but there was at least one other songwriter at the time who seemed even a better writer. That was Bob Dylan, the young American from the wilds of northern Minnesota who had gotten his start in folk music before adding electric guitars and cranking out rock and roll filled with amazing images. Dylan had survived withering criticism that he was cheapening folk music; he was confident enough in his ability to keep playing rock. Dylan and Lennon met in

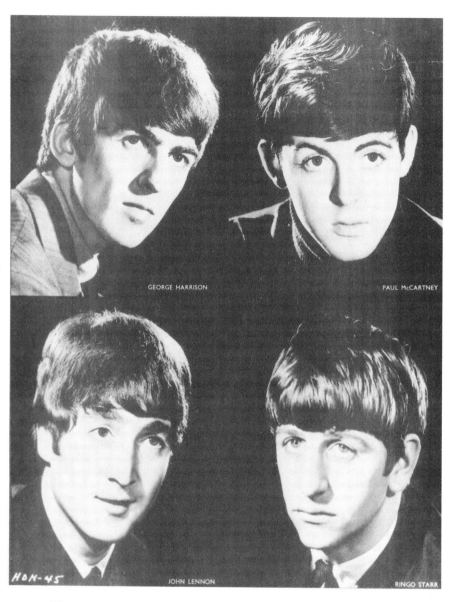

GEORGE HARRISON

PAUL McCARTNEY

JOHN LENNON

RINGO STARR

HDN-45

These are the official "mug shots" from the 1964 movie, *A Hard Day's Night.*

1964, shortly after a Dylan album, *Bringing It All Back Home*, had been released. Lennon played the album frequently.

The other meeting of note would take place a year later on America's West Coast. Brian Epstein helped arrange for the Beatles to meet Elvis Presley while the band was on a United States tour. Presley had influenced the quartet greatly. Although he had not had a rock and roll hit in several years, he still starred in a number of movies. The Beatles all urged "the King" to do more recording. He pointed out that his movie commitments made it difficult to spend much time in the studio. After a few other pleasantries, the quartet departed. Presley resented English groups for having buried his music, and the Beatles felt as if they still had not met the rock pioneer. "Where's Elvis?" became a familiar question Lennon would pose afterward.[1]

Like Presley, the Beatles had another motion-picture commitment. The shooting of their second feature, *Help!*, began in the Bahamas early in 1965. Unlike *A Hard Day's Night*, this motion picture was in color. It was shot in only nine weeks in the Bahamas and Europe and had more of a plot—though not much. A mad scientist was in search of a valuable ring, which ended up on one of Starr's fingers. There were several narrow escapes and frantic chases patterned after the James Bond spy movies, which were popular at the time. Lennon offended Bahamian officials by pointing out that a hospital, where part of the movie was briefly filmed, was filthy and that the disabled people there needed better care. This may not have been his first public display of a social conscience, but it was among his best.[2]

The film crew and the Beatles moved to wintry Austria to finish up the picture. Lennon was eating, drinking, and smoking heavily. He also was using marijuana almost every day, an illegal form of recreation he learned during his meeting with Bob Dylan. Lennon alternated between periods of lively political and philosophical discussions with friends and times when he was moody. He looked back on this time as his "Fat Elvis" period, grumbling to Cynthia that he had lost his ability to write. In contrast, his wife believed that this was the peak of his songwriting career.[3] In fact, "Help!" was such a powerful song that the name of the movie was changed after Lennon first sang it.

Lennon's complaints about loss of ability simply are not valid. Among the many memorable songs he composed in 1965 are "Norwegian Wood" and "In My Life," both on the Beatles' sixth album, *Rubber Soul.* If the group had something to complain about, it continued to be a brutal schedule that squeezed rather than coaxed their creativity. In addition to a second United States tour, the band was booked for separate tours in Europe and in Great Britain. In the studio, songs were being produced more slowly as more

John Lennon gives directions to a shivering swimmer in *Help!* The Beatles' second movie was filmed in 1965.

instruments, voices, and techniques were added to each tune. The Beatles once recorded eleven songs in a single day. Now they were down to one or two. Lennon felt a real crunch because his second book was due at the publisher's in February 1965.[4]

Perhaps the only way to get the original Beatle's attention at this time was to compliment his voice. In contrast to Paul McCartney, who sounded smooth and in control, Lennon's voice was raw and untrained. George Martin, who produced many of the Beatles' biggest hits, recalls pointing out individual songs to Lennon, songs that Martin liked because of the power of Lennon's voice. Lennon was astounded that anyone could distinguish him on a record.[5] He was equally insecure about his guitar-playing, perhaps because of his inability to read music. He was the group's rhythm guitarist. Those who play a guitar know that it is easier to play rhythm and sing than it is to play melody or harmony while vocalizing. Clearly, despite the world-wide fame, John Lennon was insecure.[6]

7

Changes

"We're more popular than Jesus now."[1]

Those words, taken from an interview published in London's *Evening Standard* newspaper in the spring of 1966, would haunt John Lennon. The British public at the time remained calm over the remark. Lennon's opinion was published in an American teenage magazine, *Datebook*, a few months later. United States reaction, two weeks before the Beatles were to begin an American tour, was maniacal. Everyone from the most pious preacher to the most bigoted member of the Ku Klux Klan staged a protest. In Georgia, fundamentalist Christians stoked a bonfire with Beatles records. Dozens of radio stations pulled some or all of the band's tunes off the air. And letters addressed "John Lennon, England" carried threats and curses.

At first, John acted disinterested.[2] Brian Epstein, who always tried to keep the Beatles' image tidy, soon asked Lennon to apologize. Epstein also feared, given the perception Americans were trigger-happy, that a lunatic would shoot Lennon as he performed. At a Chicago news conference at the start of the tour, Lennon noted, "I just said what I said and it was wrong. Or it was taken wrong. . . . if you want me to apologize, if that will make you happy, then OK, I'm sorry."[3]

Their third tour of the United States would be the last one as a group. In fact, the final Beatles performance on a stage, before an audience, took place on August 29, 1966, at Candlestick Park in San Francisco. All four band members were becoming frazzled by live performances, which had degenerated into unruly scenes where the music could hardly be heard, despite the use of huge amplifiers and booming speakers. Riots preceding and following concerts in the Philippines and in Japan, together with heavyhanded treatment by security personnel, made the band realize that they only wanted to play in the safety, comfort, and quiet of a recording studio. Besides, Lennon and in particular Harrison disliked flying, a necessary part of any tour.

Lennon returned home to stacks of mail continuing to criticize his remark about Jesus. To complicate matters, his father, Alf Lennon, had shown up at his door. John Lennon soon purchased his father a cottage and sent him money each month, despite resenting the man's long absence and unannounced arrival. Alf wanted to marry a nineteen-year-old college student, who was hired briefly by Cynthia as a secretary. Though John did not show it, he was embarrassed when his father released a horrid pop record, "That's My Life." To make matters worse, Lennon was moody, wondering what he would do if and when the Beatles broke up.[4]

Later, Lennon would recall, "I was too scared to break away from the Beatles, but I'd been looking to it since . . . we stopped touring."[5]

Because the four were so popular, they continued to be bombarded with offers. One Lennon accepted involved acting without Harrison, McCartney, or Starr in a film titled *How I Won the War*. Lennon was aware of growing opposition to the war in Vietnam at the time, and he was pleased to play the part of Private Gripweed for Richard Lester, who directed the earlier Beatles' films. Calling himself ". . . an apprentice [actor] in the middle of professionals," Lennon went to Germany initially for the filming.[6] There, his hair was cut short, and he was given a pair of "granny glasses" to wear in the movie, which also filmed in Spain. The spectacles would become a Lennon trademark and a huge fad.

On his return to London, John took Cynthia to a dinner party at the home of a dentist. George Harrison and his girlfriend, model Patty Boyd, also were there. Unknown to the guests, LSD, a powerful hallucinogen nicknamed acid, was slipped into their drinks. The

John Lennon was the only Beatles' member to appear in *How I Won the War*, a movie shot in 1966 in Spain. The film told of World War I and was where Lennon first tried—and liked—wire-rimmed "granny glasses."

substance had a strong effect on Lennon. In addition to marijuana consumption, the twenty-six-year-old million-aire now began to take large amounts of LSD. Despite Cynthia's concerns, he ate infrequently, becoming frighteningly thin. Lennon's wife put up with his drinking bouts, but use of psychedelic (mind-altering) drugs greatly bothered her.

Lennon liked going out at night, and Cynthia preferred staying at home. So it was not unusual for the rock star to hop in his chauffeur-driven car and head for a London art gallery on November 9, 1966, for a private showing recommended by singers Marianne Faithfull and Mick Jagger of the Rolling Stones. The exhibit offered strange paintings and a catalog filled with unusual items available by mail that might or might not have existed. Lennon was not sure he liked the strange exhibit but eventually was introduced to the artist, a small woman dressed all in black named Yoko Ono.

Yoko was already well known in the international artistic community by the time she and Lennon met. Like Lennon, she was married, and she was the mother of a young daughter, Kyoko. Born in Japan in 1933, Ono was the daughter of a wealthy banker. Her father moved the family to New York City when she was nineteen, and she attended Sarah Lawrence College but left without graduating. Ono held concerts in lofts in New York's Greenwich Village, where artists gathered. She toured Japan with other artists, presenting musicals based on random choices. One such performance featured a dozen radios, each tuned to a different station. She gave other performances, at Carnegie Hall and elsewhere, before heading for London in 1966 to perform and show her work.

"She taught me to think again . . ." Lennon would explain later.[7] At first, the founder of the Beatles wanted only to become Ono's patron—to sponsor her shows and produce her music. But several things appealed to Lennon about Ono: She was a woman operating successfully in a man's world; she was a Japanese person in the Western world; and she presented playful or humorous or thoughtful films, recordings, and other artistic ventures that were radical, even for the 1960s. Yet Lennon felt that "Yoko and I were on the same wavelength right from the start."[8]

Before that wavelength could be explored, Lennon had to deal with other events. Among them was work on the band's most grueling yet successful album, *Sgt. Pepper's Lonely Hearts Club Band.* The Beatles spent seven hundred hours, from the fall of 1966 to the spring of 1967, getting the tunes just right.[9] The band finished up the album, saw to it that thousands of dollars were spent on the album cover, and waited nervously for the public's verdict.

The year 1967 featured the summer of love, which was hippiedom at its height in the United States and abroad. The appropriately bearded, mustachioed or

Lennon plays a doorman at a London club as part of a brief appearance on a British television comedy show in 1966.

otherwise shaggy Beatles communicated directly to millions of young people all over the world who were becoming advocates of peace, love, and various drugs. "Lucy in the Sky With Diamonds," written by Lennon after seeing one of his son's drawings, was interpreted as being about hallucinations or LSD. Lennon later admitted that the album represented a peak in the Beatles' career, but noted that his best work may have been on the previous album, *Rubber Soul*, which featured such haunting tunes as "Eleanor Rigby." Nevertheless, the popularity of *Sgt. Pepper* could not be denied.

After all the tough recording sessions, George Harrison got the other band members interested in Eastern religion. He had been attracted to it by the music produced from a sitar, a guitarlike Indian instrument. John and Cynthia Lennon joined others at a lecture on transcendental meditation in the summer of 1967, given by Maharishi Mahesh Yogi, a meditation teacher. The following day, the Beatles and their wives traveled by train from London to Wales to spend a weekend in meditation with the Maharishi. Unfortunately, Cynthia missed the train. Lennon could have stepped off the railroad car as it slowly pulled out of London's Euston Station, but he stayed aboard.

Before the Beatles' weekend in Wales was over, they were receiving frantic messages from London: The body of Brian Epstein had been found in his apartment. Apparently, the thirty-two-year-old manager was the victim of a drug overdose. Just before his death, Epstein tried without success to convince the band to go on another tour. Lennon would later admit, "The Beatles were finished when Eppy died. I knew, deep inside me, that that was it. Without him, we'd had it."[10]

Ever since their meeting at her exhibition, Yoko Ono had stayed in contact with Lennon. She sent him cards and notes, she showed up at his house, she once virtually jumped onto the laps of John and Cynthia as they pulled away from the curb in their chauffeur-driven Rolls-Royce—now painted in psychedelic colors. More than once, Cynthia asked John if he was involved with the artist. More than once, Lennon dismissed her worries, blaming Ono's attention on the fact that she was a strange, avant-garde artist. While in India, he continued to deny his wife's suspicions. The Beatles had gone to Asia to study meditation, and Lennon was sent numerous letters from Ono.

"I was starting to drift from the Beatles before Yoko," Lennon told an interviewer in 1980. "What I did . . . in my own cowardly way was *use* Yoko . . . it was like now I have the strength to leave."[11]

Nevertheless, Lennon soon was busy helping launch Apple, the Beatles' new recording company. He suggested to Cynthia that she join several friends who were headed for a vacation in Greece. Cynthia left, returning two weeks later to find John's boyhood friend, Peter Shotton, with an embarrassed look on his face in the Lennon living room. She looked a bit further and found John and Yoko Ono in dressing gowns in an adjoining room.[12] Cynthia ran upstairs, hastily packed a few clean things, and ran out of the house to the apartment of a friend. Lennon told Peter Shotton that he was going to look for a new place where he and the love of his life, Yoko Ono, would live.[13]

8

John and Yoko

Cynthia Lennon filed for divorce on August 22, 1968, and her divorce was granted less than three months later. John hardly noticed, since it was a very busy time in his life. No wonder he did not contest the divorce but agreed to adequately support his first wife and their child, Julian.

What was on Lennon's mind at the time, besides regular amounts of alcohol, various illegal drugs, and nicotine? In fairness to the man who formed the Beatles, he believed that Yoko Ono brought out his old, more genuine, artistic, Liverpool self. Once again he was overbearing, opinionated, irreverent, a rebellious activist, and a generous donor to every charity or left-wing underdog with a cause who happened to turn up.[1] It is ironic that he felt more like himself, since Ono's crowd of artists were not known for being genuine, down-to-earth types. Ono pointed out to Lennon that the art world was filled with people who had big plans but whose plans sometimes failed to materialize.

Meanwhile, the other Beatles were pinning their hopes on their new business, Apple. Conceived as a way to invest in new talent and in everything related to recording, the idea was endorsed by everyone but Lennon. Part of Lennon's problem was that McCartney had stepped into the leadership vacuum created by the death of Brian Epstein, and Lennon was a bit resentful and jealous.[2] If McCartney was being bossy, Lennon was breaking a long-standing Beatles tradition—no one except the Beatles and necessary technicians were ever allowed in the recording studio. Now, in 1968, Lennon brought Ono with him. She sat on a speaker and criticized the way the quartet performed!

The Beatles were recording the *White Album* at the time, an important work that would have to hold its own after the immense success of *Sgt. Pepper*. Not only were Harrison, McCartney, and Starr rude to Ono, but the Apple staff of secretaries and recording technicians also treated her coldly. This made Lennon bitter, since he was obsessed with Ono.[3] Their first artistic joint venture showed their mutual interest: In June 1968 they planted two acorns, one facing east and one facing west, as part of the National Sculpture Exhibition in London. Acorns, intended for planting, were sent to a number of

John Lennon (right), George Harrison (left), and an unidentified man stroll through a street in northern India in local clothing in 1968. The Beatles went to India to take a two-month meditation camp, which made interest in meditation briefly soar in the West.

world leaders. Meant to symbolize their meeting, the twin-acorn event caused the cynical news media to think that Lennon was teetering on the edge of reality.

There were other artistic events, which were a sign that Lennon was no longer moping around the house. He and Ono released 360 white, helium-filled balloons to announce their engagement, even though neither was divorced. Each balloon contained a message urging the finder to write to Lennon at a London art gallery. Many of the letters that came back criticized his new lifestyle. Critics disliked Lennon's new approach, too. When John and Yoko released their first album, *Unfinished Music No. 1: Two Virgins*, the effort was ridiculed. The album jacket caused immense controversy—the two were photographed totally nude. They were shot frontally nude for the front of the album and nude from behind for the back. Some authorities thought the albums pornographic, and they were confiscated by law officers from New Jersey to South Africa.

What was going through Lennon's head? Obviously, he was very much in love, and he was willing to make a fool of himself for love or for peace.[4] For one reason or another, John Lennon could not seem to keep himself out of the news. While he and Yoko were living in a borrowed apartment, their sleep was interrupted by several police officers. The police rapped on the window, showed a warrant, and went through the apartment in search of illegal drugs. Because Lennon was an active drug-user, the police came away with quite a bit of evidence. It included hashish (a potent form of marijuana), illegal pills, and a small amount of morphine, a painkiller. Lennon and Ono were arrested and he was fined $207 for possession of an illegal substance.[5]

While the music of John and Yoko was being panned and the music of the Beatles was being cheered, Ono suffered a miscarriage. Lennon stayed with her in the hospital round the clock, sleeping in the bed next to her when it was available and sleeping on the floor when it was not. Lennon ceased to take care of himself during this period in November 1968. It was then that a friend asked, "Which one of you had the miscarriage?"[6] Actually, Lennon was under a great deal of pressure—he wanted to rid himself of the traditional Beatles association and jointly succeed with Ono as a performing artist.

No sooner had the news of the drug arrest and the miscarriage died down than Lennon became an antiwar activist. He had expressed sentiments against the Vietnam War several years earlier, but Brian Epstein had convinced him to keep quiet so as not to rile America, where prowar people were running the country. Now, in 1969, Lennon led demonstrations, gave money to several antiwar causes, and participated in protests designed to draw attention to the killing in Southeast Asia. Almost as an afterthought, he and Ono flew to the island of

John Lennon in 1969 led demonstrations and gave money to several antiwar causes.

Gibraltar and were quickly married on March 20, 1969. The honeymoon was among the most memorable such events ever.

Lennon called what followed "advertisements for peace," and they were at least that.[7] The newly married duo flew from Gibraltar to Paris, where they had lunch with famed artist Salvador Dali, then on to Amsterdam. There, John and Yoko decided to hold something called a "bed-in for peace." News photographers were invited to the Lennon-Ono hotel room, where they believed they were going to behold some sort of X-rated performance. Instead, John and Yoko announced that they were staying in bed for seven days on behalf of the concept of peace. The interviews the pair gave became the "B" side of their latest long-playing record, *The Wedding Album*. Besides a record, the package contained a copy of the marriage certificate and a photo of the cake.

Two months later, the couple staged their second bed-in, this one in Montreal. They had gone to Canada in part because Lennon had been refused admission to the United States as a result of his earlier drug conviction. Again, Lennon and Ono made a recording, but this time it was the memorable "Give Peace a Chance." Adding varying degrees of music or hubbub to the background were former college teacher and LSD proponent Timothy Leary, entertainer Tommy

John Lennon and Yoko Ono get out of bed in Amsterdam during their 1969 honeymoon to receive a bicycle, apparently a wedding present. Lennon and Ono were married a few days earlier in a swift ceremony on the island of Gibraltar.

Smothers, members of an East Indian temple, and Murray "the K" Kaufman, a New York City disc jockey.

As part of their peace campaign, Lennon and Ono also staged what they termed bag-ins. They appeared on stage at various performances and demonstrations but remained inside a large, usually white, bag together. Their voices could be heard, but since no one could see them, there was no way to confirm whether the contents of the bags contained the famed pair or someone else. What did it all mean? Half of the media made fun of them, which did not seem to bother Lennon a bit.[8] The other half, obviously fans of Lennon's music or persons who had turned against the war, praised any sort of Lennon involvement.

It was sometimes hard to tell if Lennon was taking his artistic stunts seriously. Just prior to Christmas 1969, he and Yoko rented billboards in a dozen major cities worldwide, proclaiming "War is over! If you want it. Happy Christmas from John and Yoko." The by-now not-so-newlyweds staged another bed-in in Canada and one in the Bahamas. The latter event ended when the couple realized how hot the weather was and got up. Their new musical group, the Plastic Ono Band, played at least one successful gig, in Canada.

All the while, Apple was losing money. It was untrue that the Beatles were going broke. In fact, by December 1968, they had earned an astonishing $154 million. But Apple Corps. was a corporation in a spin. To his credit,

John and Yoko staged their "bed-in for peace" on June 6, 1969, in Montreal. Lennon later said the bed-ins were commercials for the peace movement.

Paul McCartney suggested a number of plans to revive both the Beatles and the company. Among his thoughts was a cruise around the world on a luxury ship with the Beatles as the entertainment. He also longed for the good old days: "I think we should get back on the road, small band, go and do the clubs."[9]

Reviving the Beatles was something that no longer interested Lennon. "I think you're daft," he told McCartney in an Apple board meeting. "I wasn't going to tell you but I'm breaking the group up. It feels good. It feels like a divorce."[10] What was not said, of course, was that Lennon and McCartney, the most successful songwriting team in rock and roll history, were growing increasingly distant. McCartney was the showman, eager to be on stage. Lennon was the artist, concerned with the quality and the originality of any kind of presentation. When the kinds of pressures on them are examined, it may be miraculous that the Beatles stayed together as long as they did. Or that, even when Lennon talked of quitting, they were producing great, two-sided hits such as McCartney's "Hey Jude" and Lennon's "Revolution."

The symbolic end to the Beatles as a group may have come with the sale of the rights to most of their music. Northern Songs, which controlled the rights to the tunes, sold them to a huge company called A.T.V. Music. Lennon was livid, even though as a stockholder he would make millions from the transaction.[11]

9

To America

Did John Lennon, despite the drugs and the drinking, the divorce and remarriage, the wacky art and the bed-ins for peace, still have what it took as a songwriter? He did, and he showed that old ability on January 27 and 28, 1970.

Lennon sat at the piano the morning of January 27, toying with three simple notes, much like the tune conceived for "All You Need Is Love." Within a few minutes, he had married words and music, and he was eager to record and release the song immediately.[1] Lennon contacted George Harrison, Billy Preston, and several other musicians, who met him that evening in an Apple studio. Also there was Phil Spector, the American record producer. Spector was skilled at adding layer after layer of sound on a record.

Spector listened to Lennon's latest and began to enhance it. He muffled some drums, amplified others, added rhythmic handclaps, and asked musicians to play instruments in more boisterous ways as he laid tape over tape over tape for a crescendo of sound. At one point, Billy Preston ran to a nearby pub, recruited several drinkers there, and in minutes had them singing hearty choruses on one of Spector's tracks!

Lennon's voice was almost overwhelmed by the sound, even though Spector had it echoing mightily. Lennon loved the finished product—and so did the public.[2] "Instant Karma," as it was called, was a smash hit. "Was the message that you could do whatever you wanted? Or that easy solutions didn't always turn out so easy? Lennon wasn't saying," a writer noted, but he could still create and perform with the best of them.[3]

His problems sometimes were of his own making. On a whim, Lennon decided to show Ono his old Liverpool neighborhood. The two toured the city in a rented car, eyeing the clubs, the schools, and the dwellings that were a part of Lennon's past. They then stopped at the home of a Lennon aunt and uncle to pick up young Julian. Driving through the Scottish Highlands, Lennon ran the rented automobile off the road, rolling it, and leaving it in a heap. He and Ono both suffered facial cuts and appeared to be bloody messes, though they were not badly hurt. Julian suffered shock. The accident says something of Lennon's driving ability. The Lennons had the demolished car hauled back to southern England, where it rested on their lawn.

At about the same time, the couple was feeling pressure from poor sales of their records and from their attempts to keep peace ideas in the headlines.[4] Lennon used heroin to escape his worries. He kicked the habit within a few months, and he wrote of the experience in a song he labeled "Cold Turkey." McCartney found the song depressing and would have nothing to do with it, so Lennon recorded it with the Plastic Ono Band. McCartney's refusal prompted Lennon to credit the song only to himself rather than use the standard Lennon/McCartney byline. Here was one more sign that the Beatles were distant and growing more so. Legal action to end the band's partnership began on December 31, 1970.

Once Mr. and Mrs. John Lennon found the home of their dreams, they decided to move. Their new place, at least for several months, was a three-hundred-year-old, $270,000 mansion called Tittenhurst Park, twenty-six miles from London. The thirty-room mansion included seventy-two acres with gardens, a farm, cottages, and several other outbuildings, plus a lodge at its entrance. The site would hardly have time to get used to the Lennons. The new owners hired members of a religious sect to help them redecorate, which may have been amusing but added nothing to the value of the property.

Yoko Ono miscarried in October 1970, and the Lennons left Britain the following July.

Lennon and Ono flew to New York, in part so that Ono could see her daughter, Kyoko. The girl was living in New York City in the custody of Ono's former husband, Anthony Cox. Ono was like Lennon in that she had to make arrangements to visit her only child. Ono knew the city well, walking Lennon around the many artsy shops and hangouts. If Lennon initially was awed by London, he was overwhelmed by New York. "I should have been born in New York," he said.[5] Obviously, he ended up liking the city a lot, particularly the avant-garde art scene. The two decided to stay, since they often needed to be there, anyway, and since Ono believed she was the object of dislike in Britain for having broken up the Beatles.[6]

There were other reasons for the move. Lennon had been studying under Arthur Janov, a psychologist who taught that people had to strip away layers of their lives in order to reach and deal with their fears. Lennon felt for a while that he made progress under Janov, having flown the psychological expert to the United Kingdom.[7] But Janov had commitments in the United States, and for maximum benefit, Lennon would have to spend time in California at Janov's institute. New York City seemed a good compromise, since it was much closer to California than England. Kyoko spent time with her mother in New York, and

Lennon and Ono believed that the city was the center of the art world.

In a particularly active period, the couple cranked out several short films. Most of them involved events such as attaching a camera to a balloon, floating the balloon as high as it would go—up through the clouds—and projecting the resulting film. Lennon and Ono helped rock legend Frank Zappa and his band, the Mothers of Invention, close New York City's old Fillmore East, the theater where so many bands had played. Ono put on an ambitious gallery exhibition in New York she called *This Is Not Here* as Lennon performed in several benefit concerts. *Imagine*, one of his classic albums, was finished in October 1971.

The two moved into a spacious hotel suite initially, then found a brownstone home in Greenwich Village. Once they got settled into the brownstone, suspicious events took place. Strange noises heard during phone conversations made Lennon and Ono wonder if there was a bug on the line. Who would want to spy on anyone as open as John Lennon? If anything, he had always been too willing to share his every thought and secret. Living at street level, even with hired security, Lennon and Ono also sometimes felt they were being spied upon, either from the street or from windows opposite them.[8] The pair spent time with several known radicals, including Jerry Rubin and Abby Hoffman. With the Vietnam War grinding on and on, the United States government had been worried for some time about alleged left-wing activity.

Fear of Lennon's power resulted in a note from the United States Senate's Judiciary Subcommittee early in 1972 to John Mitchell, President Richard M. Nixon's attorney general. Senator Strom Thurmond of South Carolina worried over disruption of the 1972 Republican National Convention, scheduled for San Diego, California. He wondered in the note if something could be done about the presence of John Lennon, a foreigner, in America. What if the wealthy Lennon financed some sort of "Dump Nixon" movement? Lennon continued to point out that the people were at the heart of political activity, and he merely wrote songs about them.[9] That failed to persuade federal authorities—on March 16, 1972, Lennon received a deportation order, based on his conviction in London in 1968 for drug possession.

The argument against sending Lennon out of the country was a simple one: Ono was in the United States, as a United States citizen, to see her daughter. Would the government split up a husband and a wife, or deprive Ono and Kyoko of periodic visits? Numerous people spoke up for Lennon, including New York's mayor at the time, John Lindsay. He called the proceedings "a grave injustice," adding that the real reason for the harassment was due to the fact that the Lennons "speak out with strong and critical voices on the major issues of the day."[10] Support for Lennon was widespread, among the famous and among everyday people on both sides of the Atlantic.

Lennon continued to tackle issues he felt were important. He attended an antiwar rally in New York City in April 1972, he gave benefit concerts for left-wing causes, and he socialized with radical people. A mediocre album, *Some Time in New York City*, appeared in June 1972, and it fanned the flames. Lennon and Ono made a number of anti-British remarks on the record, which was not offered for sale in England until mid-September. Nevertheless, Lord Harlech, the former British ambassador to the United States, spoke up for Lennon on July 4, America's Independence Day.[11]

John Lennon's attorney obtained a six-month delay in the proceedings while he tried to prove that the United States government was picking on his client. Though the case would not be finished until the fall of 1975, Lennon finally won his green card after a special Court of Appeal decision. The court told the Immigration Service that it could not consider Lennon's 1968 marijuana conviction in England and that the service could not discriminate against the music star because of his political activity. Lennon's attorney advised him not to crow about the decision.

The Lennons moved into the Dakota, a landmark New York City apartment building, late in 1972. The Dakota was a cooperative apartment building—members

John Lennon and Yoko Ono perform at a Madison Square Garden concert in 1972. This was part of a larger benefit concert on behalf of retarded children.

had to vote their approval to let the Lennons buy in. Initially, they rented the apartment of actor Robert Ryan. They were admitted, and the couple made the ten-room apartment their home, decorating it almost exclusively in white. With a permanent address, what would the future bring?

10

Journey's End

After three miscarriages and consulting an ancient Chinese herbalist and after giving up every drug but cigarettes, Lennon and Ono were rewarded with a child. Sean Taro Ono Lennon was born on October 9, 1972. ("Sean" is "John" in the Irish language of Gaelic, while "Taro" means "John," or close to it, in Japanese). The date was Lennon's thirty-second birthday, marked by a dangerous delivery for Yoko Ono, who needed a blood transfusion. Sean arrived by cesarean section. The boy's famous father was there through it all. Looking back, Lennon may have considered himself lucky to be around.

In October 1973, John and Yoko split up. They had been getting on each other's nerves for some time, which probably was natural since they were never out of each

John Lennon, with his hair closely cropped, in 1973. He and Yoko
Ono would soon break up.

other's sight. At any rate, Lennon went to Los Angeles and hooked up with several musician friends, including Harry Nilsson, Keith Moon of the Who, and fellow former Beatle Ringo Starr. It was, Lennon recalled, "the lost weekend that lasted eighteen months."[1]

What had happened to one of the great romances of the century? "I thought I had to 'move on' again because I was suffering being with John," Ono said.[2] The pressure of being married to a famous rocker was causing her distress. Ono felt that separation was the only solution. "We talked about it and she kicked me out is what actually happened," according to Lennon.[3]

"Well, first I thought, Whoopee! . . . And then I woke up one day and thought . . . I want to go home. But she wouldn't let me come home. That's why it was eighteen months instead of six. . . . I was just insane."[4]

A curious set of events brought John and Yoko back together. Despite his behavior on the West Coast, Lennon continued to write and record songs. In November 1974, "Whatever Gets You Thru The Night" topped the *Billboard* single-record chart. Elton John had played keyboard on the record, and he made Lennon promise to join him at a concert if the record reached number one. Lennon kept his promise, appearing during Elton John's Thanksgiving Day show in New York City. Ono was in the audience—at Elton's suggestion—and her heart must have gone out to her husband. John returned to New York for good early in 1975, moved back into the Dakota, and soon learned that he and Yoko might be parents again.[5]

"I am going to be forty, and life begins at forty, so they promise. Oh, I *believe* it, too. Because I feel fine. *Wow!* What's going to happen next?"[6]

A restless soul, Lennon was happy with himself and his situation as he turned forty. But he was still a man of strong opinions. For example, he refused to listen to Beatles' music, feeling that every song could have been done better. He also refused to take credit for how rock and roll took shape, pointing out that all rock is built on what has been played and sung before. But his strongest feelings were reserved for people who continued to ask, a decade later, if the Beatles would reunite. " 'Can you do it again?' No way! You can't do things twice."[7]

Those thoughts, from a booklength interview conducted by a *Playboy* magazine writer in 1980, indicate that John Lennon had come out of his shell. After performing the kinds of tasks around the house that many unknown mothers and father have always done, Lennon felt his ability sufficiently returned to create new songs. "My spirit moved me to write suddenly, which I haven't done in a long, long time,"[8] he told *Playboy.*

What was Ono up to from 1975 to 1980 while John played the role of mother and father to their young son? As Lennon pointed out, she was making a great deal of money by managing their affairs. "When I was cleaning the cat (litter) and feeding Sean, she was sitting in rooms full of smoke with men in three-piece suits they couldn't button."[9] Ono was busy buying and selling everything from priceless antiques to real estate and prize cattle, the result being that the Lennon-Ono money pile was virtually as big as ever. With their business life under control, Lennon and Ono used their spare moments beginning in 1980 to write a batch of songs. The result was *Double Fantasy*, the first album by either since Lennon's *Walls and Bridges* in 1974.

Double Fantasy was offered to the public on November 17, 1980. Critics who longed for the raw voice of the old John Lennon were somewhat disappointed, since his voice on every cut was smoothly double-tracked. They also found his seven songs more sentimental than the seven of Ono's, leading to guesses that Ono had the upper hand in the marriage and was running matters. But others saw the album, which included such hits as "Starting Over" and "Nobody Told Me," as the product of two complex people whose relationship had survived tough times.[10] Among the thousands of eager Lennon fans to purchase the album was a young man named Mark David Chapman.

Chapman was a Georgia native who had held a string of poor-paying jobs in Hawaii, where the twenty-five-year-old lived with his wife. One of his jobs had been that of a security guard; he had learned to fire a handgun because he sometimes carried one when in uniform. The mentally disturbed Chapman had for years been racked by voices that he believed to be alternately from God and from the devil. The voices were sometimes insistent, leading the young man to believe an important event in his future would result in the triumph of either good or evil.[11]

Chapman read an *Esquire* magazine article about John Lennon that was far from flattering. It noted that Lennon talked of peace, love, and revolution while living the life of a millionaire. In short, the article implied, Lennon was a phony. Phonies were despised by Chapman after he read J. D. Salinger's classic 1950 novel, *Catcher in the Rye*.[12] The hero of the book is obsessed with protecting children and doing away with phonies, though all he does is daydream that he is shooting people he dislikes. Chapman armed himself with a handgun and flew to New York City. He rented a hotel room near the Dakota and went looking for John Lennon.

A freelance photographer pointed Lennon out to the deranged young man, who was carrying a copy of Lennon's *Double Fantasy* album. Chapman asked Lennon to autograph the album jacket, and Lennon obliged. The rock star then got into a limousine and was whisked safely away—for the time being. Clad in several layers of clothes to ward off the cold, Chapman hung around the Dakota's entrance, chatting off and on for several hours with the doorman. That night, as Lennon and Ono stepped out of their limousine, Chapman followed them toward the door. He pulled his five-shot gun and fired repeatedly, the first two bullets striking Lennon in the back. Lennon spun and staggered into the lobby, where he fell. Though police came immediately, Lennon could not be resuscitated and died in a nearby hospital.

His killer threw the gun on the sidewalk and hung around until police arrived. He whined as they pushed him against a wall, handcuffed him, and drove off with the young suspect. Chapman initially entered a plea of not guilty. He later changed the plea, after reporting that God told him to do so, and was sentenced to twenty years to life, first at Rikers Island and then in the big, upstate New York prison at Attica. Chapman has attempted to contact Yoko Ono by mail on several occasions, but she does not acknowledge his letters. Apparently, the killer cannot grasp the seriousness of his crime.

John Lennon's life continued to have widespread influence after his death. Within three weeks of the shooting, "(Just Like) Starting Over" had sold more than one million copies, and *Double Fantasy* became America's top-selling album. "Imagine" was the fastest-selling record in Britain in January 1981, and more than 2 million Lennon records were sold in Great Britain in the two months following Lennon's death. Ono spent thousands of dollars placing full-page ads in newspapers in six countries "In Gratitude" for the kind thoughts of fans. Yet Lennon's life and death had longer-running and more important consequences.

Into the 1990s, the phrase "Give Peace a Chance" would draw a line between those who continue to hope for a peaceful world and those who cynically sneered at such an idea. Many artists, from George Harrison to Paul McCartney to Elton John to Queen to Pink Floyd composed and sang songs in Lennon's memory. Numerous books were published, ranging from the lengthy interviews Lennon did for *Playboy* magazine just before his death to *The Ballad of John and Yoko*, written by the editors of *Rolling Stone*. Libraries to this day carry a number of books about the fallen rock star and peace activist. Librarians indicate that the books are heavily read.

Not everyone treated Ono well. She continued to amass a huge personal fortune, but several people who respected her husband did not care for her or her view of art and spread stories that were exaggerated or untrue. Several scandalous books and articles were published, including *Dakota Days*, by John Green. Green was a tarot card reader who had once forecast the future for Ono. Yet Lennon's wife continued to share what she had, donating $100,000 in 1984 to the Salvation Army's Strawberry Field children's home in Liverpool. Books, pictures, manuscripts, and trinkets by or about Lennon

Fans of John Lennon stand in front of the Dakota, the scene of his murder, on December 14, 1980. A silent memorial vigil was held later in the day.

continued to sell well, as did songs that had not been released at the time of his death.

As John Lennon drifted from popular memory, his high clear voice was heard once again—with the Beatles. Lennon in 1979 had recorded "Free as a Bird," a song about family that he intended for a rock opera, *The Ballad of John and Yoko.*[13] George Harrison, Paul McCartney, and Ringo Starr added their voices and instruments to it in 1995 and the tune became part of a new Beatles album. This *Anthology* early in 1996 had climbed to the top of the *Billboard* magazine sales list.[14]

Combined with a six-hour Beatles documentary aired on ABC-TV over three prime-time evenings, the album was an answer to the question: "When are the Beatles going to get back together?" In a new and electronic way, they had. Sadly, John Lennon, the founder of the most famous musical group of all time, was unaware of the reunion. Some fans heard "Free as a Bird," a light and happy tune, and waited eagerly for the Beatles' many hours of unreleased Abbey Road recording studio material to be collected and offered to the public. In that way, John Lennon will be with us all for quite some time.

Chronology

1940—Born in Liverpool, England, on October 9.

1945—Starts grade school in Liverpool.

1952—Begins Quarry Bank High School.

1957—Lennon and others form a musical group, the Quarry Men, in May; Paul McCartney joins the group in July; Lennon enters Liverpool College of Art, September.

1958—George Harrison joins the Quarry Men in February.

1960—The group changes its name to the Beatles on June 2.

1961—The Beatles' first single, *My Bonnie*, by Tony Sheridan, with backing by the Beatles, is released in Germany.

1962—Manager Brian Epstein and the Beatles sign with the EMI record label; Ringo Starr joins the Beatles on August 18; Lennon marries Cynthia Powell on August 23; the Beatles record their first single, "Love Me Do," on September 4.

1963—A son, John Charles Julian, is born to John and Cynthia on April 8; the Beatles' first album, *Please Please Me*, tops the charts in England.

1964—"I Want to Hold Your Hand" tops the singles charts in the United States on February 1; 73 million viewers see the Beatles on *The Ed Sullivan Show* February 9; the Beatles begin shooting their first movie, *A Hard Day's Night*, March 2; Lennon's first book, *In His Own Write*, is published on March 23.

1965—*A Spaniard in the Works*, Lennon's second book, is published on June 24; the second Beatles' feature film, *Help!*, debuts on July 29.

1966—Lennon tells a London newspaper that the Beatles are more popular than Jesus; filming of *How I Won the War* begins in Germany on September 6; Lennon meets Japanese artist Yoko Ono in London on November 9.

1967—*Sgt. Pepper's Lonely Hearts Club Band* album is released, June 1.

1968—*Yellow Submarine*, the Beatles' cartoon film, debuts in London on July 17; Cynthia Lennon and John are divorced; he pleads guilty to marijuana possession and is fined.

1969—Lennon and Yoko Ono are married on March 20 and begin their weeklong "bed-in for peace" in Amsterdam March 25; John and Yoko record *Give Peace a Chance* while in bed.

1970—Paul McCartney announces that he is leaving the Beatles; the Beatles' final film, *Let It Be*, premieres in New York on May 13.

1971—Lennon releases his *Imagine* album, October 8.

1972—Their United States visas expired, Lennon and Ono begin the battle against deportation; Yoko Ono gives birth to their only child, Sean Taro Ono Lennon, October 9.

1973—Lennon and Ono separate after four and a half years of marriage; John heads to Los Angeles; Lennon's *Mind Games* album is released, November 16.

1974—Lennon's *Walls and Bridges* album is released, October 4.

1975—Lennon returns to New York and is is reunited with Ono.

1976—Lennon becomes a legal United States citizen.

1977—The Lennons attend the inauguration of President Jimmy Carter, January 20.

1980—Lennon and Ono's comeback album, *Double Fantasy*, is released; Lennon is shot to death on a New York City street on December 8; worldwide ten-minute vigil in Lennon's honor takes place on December 14.

Selected Discography

(These recordings and their release dates are for the United States only; singles and albums in Great Britain and elsewhere may have differed slightly in content and date of release.)

With the Beatles

"My Bonnie/The Saints" (The Beatles with Tony Sheridan, Polydor, 1962).

"Please Please Me/Ask Me Why" (Vee Jay, 1963).

Introducing the Beatles (Vee Jay, 1963).

Meet the Beatles (Capitol, 1964).

A Hard Day's Night (United Artists, 1964).

Help! (Capitol, 1965).

Revolver (Capitol, 1965).

Sgt. Pepper's Lonely Hearts Club Band (Capitol, 1967).

Magical Mystery Tour (Capitol, 1967).

Yellow Submarine (Apple, 1969).

Anthology (Apple/Capitol, 1995).

Solo

Give Peace a Chance/Remember Love (Single, Apple, 1969).

Imagine (Apple, 1971).

Rock 'N' Roll (Apple, 1975).

Shaved Fish (Apple, 1975).

With Yoko Ono

Unfinished Music No. 1: Two Virgins (Apple, 1968).

Double Fantasy (Geffen, 1980).

With the Plastic Ono Band

Live Peace in Toronto 1969 (Apple, 1969).

John Lennon: Plastic Ono Band (Apple, 1970).

Chapter Notes

Chapter 1

1. Albert Goldman, *The Lives of John Lennon* (New York: William Morrow and Company, 1988), p. 153.

2. Ray Coleman, *Lennon: The Definitive Biography* (New York: HarperCollins, 1992), p. 71.

3. Ibid.

4. Peter Brown and Steven Gaines, *The Love You Make: An Insider's Story of The Beatles* (New York: McGraw-Hill, 1983), p. 122.

Chapter 2

1. Albert Goldman, *The Lives of John Lennon* (New York: William Morrow and Company, 1988), p. 32.

2. Ibid., pp. 34–35.

3. Ray Coleman, *Lennon: The Definitive Biography* (New York: HarperCollins, 1992), p. 89.

4. Ibid., p. 91.

5. Ibid.

6. Carole Lynn Corbin, *John Lennon* (New York: Franklin Watts, 1982), p. 12.

7. Goldman, pp. 48–49.

8. David Sheff, *The Playboy Interviews With John Lennon and Yoko Ono* (New York: Playboy Press, 1981), p. 138.

9. Coleman, p. 105.

10. Ibid., p. 108.

11. Sheff, p. 48.

Chapter 3

1. David Sheff, *The Playboy Interviews With John Lennon and Yoko Ono* (New York: Playboy Press, 1981), p. 48.

2. Albert Goldman, *The Lives of John Lennon* (New York: William Morrow and Company, 1988), p. 62.

3. Ibid., p. 63.

4. Sheff, p. 117.

5. Ibid., p. 126.

6. Carole Lynn Corbin, *John Lennon* (New York: Franklin Watts, 1982), pp. 19–20.

7. Lloyd Rose, "Long Gone John: Lennon and the Revelations," in *The Lennon Companion: Twenty-five Years of Comment*, ed. by Elizabeth Thomson and David Gutman (New York: Schirmer Books, 1987), p. 17.

8. Ray Coleman, *Lennon: The Definitive Biography* (New York: HarperCollins, 1992), pp. 73–74.

9. Goldman, pp. 81–82.

10. Coleman, pp. 197–198.

11. Sheff, pp. 140–141.

12. Goldman, p. 174.

Chapter 4

1. Ray Coleman, *Lennon: The Definitive Biography* (New York: HarperCollins, 1992), p. 206

2. Carole Lynn Corbin, *John Lennon* (New York: Franklin Watts, 1982), pp. 28–29.

3. Coleman, pp. 28–29.

4. Ibid., p. 245.

5. Ibid.

6. Ibid., p. 248.

7. Albert Goldman, *The Lives of John Lennon* (New York: William Morrow and Company, 1988), p. 118.

8. Coleman, p. 252.

9. Ibid., p. 258.

10. David Sheff, *The Playboy Interviews With John Lennon and Yoko Ono* (New York: Playboy Press, 1981), p. 142.

11. Ibid., p. 131.

12. Coleman, p. 263.

13. Ibid.

Chapter 5

1. Richard Buskin, *The Beatles: Memories and Memorabilia* (New York: Crescent Books, 1994), p. 4.

2. Ibid.

3. Ray Coleman, *Lennon: The Definitive Biography* (New York: HarperCollins, 1992), pp. 273–274.

4. Ibid., p. 290.

5. Ibid., p. 293.

6. Ibid., p. 294.

7. Ibid., p. 295.

8. Ibid., p. 296.

9. Ibid., pp. 298–299.

10. Ibid., pp. 304–305.

11. Albert Goldman, *The Lives of John Lennon* (New York: William Morrow and Company, 1988), pp. 143–144.

Chapter 6

1. Albert Goldman, *The Lives of John Lennon* (New York: William Morrow and Company, 1988), pp. 181–182.

2. Ray Coleman, *Lennon: The Definitive Biography* (New York: HarperCollins, 1992), p. 346.

3. Ibid., p. 348.

4. Carole Lynn Corbin, *John Lennon* (New York: Franklin Watts, 1982), p. 60.

5. Coleman, pp. 369–370.

6. Ibid., p. 370.

Chapter 7

1. Carole Lynn Corbin, *John Lennon* (New York: Franklin Watts, 1982), p. 61.

2. Ray Coleman, *Lennon: The Definitive Biography* (New York: HarperCollins, 1992), p. 405.

3. Ibid., p. 408.

4. Albert Goldman, *The Lives of John Lennon* (New York: William Morrow and Company, 1988), pp. 287–292.

5. David Sheff, *The Playboy Interviews With John Lennon and Yoko Ono* (New York: Playboy Press, 1981), p. 40.

6. Coleman, p. 413.

7. Anthony Fawcett, *John Lennon: One Day at a Time* (New York: Grove Press, 1976), p. 27.

8. Ibid.

9. Coleman, p. 425.

10. Ibid., p. 433.

11. Sheff, p. 130.

12. Coleman, pp. 435–438.

13. Ibid., pp. 436–437.

Chapter 8

1. Albert Goldman, *The Lives of John Lennon* (New York: William Morrow and Company, 1988), p. 288.

2. Ray Coleman, *Lennon: The Definitive Biography* (New York: HarperCollins, 1992), p. 452.

3. David Sheff, *The Playboy Interviews With John Lennon and Yoko Ono* (New York: Playboy Press, 1981), pp. 122–123.

4. Anthony Fawcett, *John Lennon: One Day at a Time* (New York: Grove Press, 1976), pp. 40–41.

5. Coleman, p. 704.

6. Ibid., p. 457.

7. Goldman, pp. 344–346.

8. Ibid., p. 346.

9. Coleman, p. 472.

10. Ibid., p. 473.

11. Ibid., pp. 477–479.

Chapter 9

1. John Robertson, *The Art & Music of John Lennon* (New York: Carol Publishing Group, 1991), pp. 121–122.

2. Ibid.

3. Ibid., p. 122.

4. Anthony Fawcett, *John Lennon: One Day at a Time* (New York: Grove Press, 1976), pp. 53–54.

5. Albert Goldman, *The Lives of John Lennon* (New York: William Morrow and Company, 1988), p. 400.

6. David Sheff, *The Playboy Interviews With John Lennon and Yoko Ono* (New York: Playboy Press, 1981), p. 122.

7. Ray Coleman, *Lennon: The Definitive Biography* (New York: HarperCollins, 1992), p. 515.

8. Jon Wiener, "John Lennon Versus the FBI," in *The Lennon Companion: Twenty-five Years of Comment,* ed. by Elizabeth Thomson and David Gutman (New York: Schirmer Books, 1987), pp. 188–197.

9. Coleman, pp. 575–576.

10. Andy Peebles, *The Lennon Tapes* (London: British Broadcasting, 1981), p. 45.

11. Coleman, pp. 716–717.

Chapter 10

1. David Sheff, *The Playboy Interviews With John Lennon and Yoko Ono* (New York: Playboy Press, 1981), p. 20.

2. Ibid., p. 24.

3. Ibid., p. 19.

4. Ibid., p. 20.

5. Ray Coleman, *Lennon: The Definitive Biography* (New York: HarperCollins, 1992), pp. 719–720.

6. Sheff, p. 7.

7. Ibid., p. 72.

8. Ibid., p. 74.

9. *Frontline*, Public Broadcasting System network show, December 6, 1995.

10. Ibid.

11. Ibid.

12. Ibid.

13. Yahlin Chang and others, "Beatlemania," *Newsweek,* October 23, 1995, pp. 57-67.

14. "Charts," *Rolling Stone,* January 25, 1996, p. 84.

Further Reading

Buskin, Richard. *The Beatles: Memories and Memorabilia.* Avenel, N.J.: Crescent Books, 1994.

Cohen, Sara. *Rock Culture in Liverpool.* New York: Clarendon Press, 1991.

Coleman, Ray. *Lennon: The Definitive Biography.* New York: HarperCollins, 1992.

Corbin, Carole Lynn. *John Lennon.* New York: Franklin Watts, 1982.

Fawcett, Anthony. *John Lennon: One Day at a Time.* New York: Grove Press, 1976.

Goldman, Albert. *The Lives of John Lennon.* New York: Bantam Books, 1989.

Green, John. *Dakota Days.* New York: St. Martin's Press, 1983.

Hertsgaard, Mark. *A Day in the Life.* New York: Delacorte Press, 1995.

Kaiser, Charles. "Eight Days a Week." *The New York Times Book Review,* May 21, 1995, 18.

Martin, George, with William Pearson. *With a Little Help From My Friends.* Boston: Little, Brown, 1995.

Peebles, Andy. *The Lennon Tapes.* London: British Broadcasting, 1981.

Robertson, John. *The Art & Music of John Lennon.* New York: Citadel Press, 1993.

Thomson, Elizabeth, and David Gutman, eds. *The Lennon Companion, Twenty-five Years of Comment.* New York: Schirmer Books, 1988.

Weiner, Jon. *Come Together, John Lennon in His Time.* New York: Random House, 1984.

Index